The Race For Life

Poems by Bryony Carr and Others

Pomegranate
BOOKS

First published in 2004 by Pomegranate Books

© 2004 Bryony Carr

Printed in Great Britain
by Biddles Ltd, King's Lynn

ISBN 1-84289-003-4

Pomegranate Books
3 Brynland Avenue, Bristol BS7 9DR, England
www.pomegranatebooks.co.uk

Dedicated to all my friends
who didn't survive

Preface

In April 1996 I was diagnosed with a brain tumour. This was to be the beginning of six years of sickness and uncertainty. It all started just three weeks before my eighteenth birthday.

It's only natural that most of us should take life for granted, but when you find yourself in a situation where this is simply not possible, you begin inevitably to change your perspectives, because cancer is a life-altering experience.

Simply feeling grateful to be alive, I wanted to express this by doing something to help others in a similar situation. So, I decided to publish a book of poems and donate the profits to charity. This seemed an appropriate option to me because a poem can reveal so much that words ordinarily cannot say, and I hope that what you read will give you some insight into the world of fighting to survive and how it is perceived by the patient and those close to them.

Mine was a specific childhood brain tumour (medulloblastoma), which most commonly occurs in children between the ages of three and eight and tends to be more prevalent in boys. 'Why me?' I thought. I am seventeen and female?

The day following the diagnosis I underwent a ten-hour operation to remove the tumour, waking up to a world of frustration and anger. I couldn't walk, talk or feed myself, communication with the big wide world had ceased, and there was the added factor of not knowing how long all this would last, if not forever.

Thankfully, the surgery was successful. After, I had a course of intensive radiotherapy, daily for seven weeks, followed by physiotherapy over the next year. This was to help me deal with unsteadiness and other co-ordination problems because the tumour had been growing in my cerebellum, the part of the brain that controls the co-ordination of muscles, balance and posture.

The next couple of years were concerned with getting my life back to normal and starting to do things that any normal eighteen-year-old would do. So, I went on to start a degree in Biomedical Sciences at the University of the West of England (UWE) in 1998 but during my first year the cancer recurred. This time my medical treatment involved chemotherapy and a bone marrow transplant.

Now in 2004 I am still alive but on medical treatment for the rest of my life. Having this kind of cancer has its consequences. The tumour affected my control over the right side of my body, so I had to learn to write with my left hand. I also had to give up my dreams of becoming a professional musician and activities that I loved such as skiing and bicycle riding. Nonetheless, I consider myself to be very lucky. Having cancer so early in life has changed me. I sense myself to be a different person now from what I was, and I hope a better one. At the risk of sounding obvious, an experience like this makes you appreciate what you have got very much more. My family are so incredibly important to me now, and my friends too. I feel that it has had the effect of making you less selfish. For example, I now consider people's feelings more when making decisions on matters that might affect them.

I joined a group known as TOPS (Teenage Oncology Patient Support) in 1997 through which I have formed a number of close friendships. One of these friends, Emma Joce, was diagnosed with Hodgkin's Disease at the age of fourteen. Emma, having another rare form of cancer has had to go through similar experiences and medical treatment to me. Our friendship means everything to me

– a bond that I hope will never be broken. She has kindly agreed for me to use one of her poems in this anthology.

I am twenty-five now and have graduated from university with an honours degree. My outlook has changed. I consider life to be rather like a 'Jack In The Box' – now it's here and then it's gone. I don't take things for granted anymore. All I really know is that you should make the most out of life; try to do what you want despite any hurdles that you may encounter and most of all try always to be happy and enjoy the time that you have in this world, whether it be six months or sixty years. The one thing we can say with certainty is that we just simply don't know.

CR

Most of the poems were written by me, some by friends; many of them penned as a source of encouragement to keep going in the face of adversity. The purpose of this book is to give the reader a sense of the inner journey I underwent, where the love and support of friends was a vital part. At times like this friends become unimaginably important. They are a life line.

Acknowledgements

I would like to thank my mother, Jill, my father, Derek, and my sister, Erica, for being around whenever I needed them.

My good friends Emma Joce, Susannah Knowles and Catherine Rossouw for allowing me to reveal their poetry skills.

My surgeon, Ian Pople, for saving my life, my consultant oncologist, Stephen Lowis, for all the medical treatment I received during my illness. All the doctors and nurses who were involved in my battle against cancer.

To Fairfield Grammar School and the University of the West of England for my education.

To CLIC (Cancer and Leukaemia in Childhood), TOPS (Teenage Oncology Patient Support) and Cancer Research UK for supporting my social and psychological needs.

A special thank you to my grandma, Lorna Howard, and to my good friend Frank Rhodes, who is currently undergoing treatment for cancer.

Poems

The Race For Life

When times are hard
Try to remember
Things always seem
Worse than they are.

Once upon a time
I used to believe
Life would be quite simple
Now I know different.

There will always be
A person to judge
A starting line
Someone to beat
A hurdle to cross
A way to run
A race to win
An event to finish.

This race I call life.

Bryony 1996

19

Dolphins

Dolphins silk creatures of the sea
Gliding free through the oceans of the world
Like a comb brushed along flowing sand

Swimming together in schools
Like a puppy staying close by his mother
Graceful wonderful forms of life

Affectionate acute
Harmonising music
Symbolising purity of soul

Bryony 1996

So White, So Blue

My toes my fingers are cold
But my face feels hot
The sun blinds me
As I traverse the testing red slope
The snow is so white
The sky so blue

Bryony 1996

What I Need To Say

I love him all the time,
We do lots of things together.
At the moment I'm very happy,
I hope it's forever.

Bryony 1996

The Things I Love

The sound of music
The smell of flowers
Love in the air
The summer sun
Stars in the heavens
Happiness
A smile for everyone

Bryony 1996

Is It There?

Can I feel it?
Is it there?
Love is blind
It's forever
I have promised him
He seems relieved

Bryony 1996

Bryony

Comfortable like a well read book
Self assured like bright red lipstick
A glass of champagne full to the top
A bright red balloon rising in the sky
A shot of brandy on a cold winter night
A chocolate milkshake, thick and satisfying
A good old gossip over the phone
A friendly hug to say hello

She has.......
A laugh like the tinkle of ice in a glass
Brown eyes that sparkle and brim with fun
A smile that lights up a dull room
A presence which is unforgettable
A heart as rich as gold
A kitten's purr of contentment

Generous, warm hearted, loving
Unique

My friend Bry

Catherine Rossouw 1996

Bry

Like a bird flying through the air
Singing out a sweet song to the world
She brings hope and freedom
To those she meets
Calm but emotional
Sharing her feelings with those around her
Taking time to decide on the right option
Always doing the best thing
Eyes shining as bright as the stars
Containing unknown depths
Sometimes hiding fear or joy but never expressionless
Sympathy if needed for those close enough to care
She has a fiery soul
With artistic temperament
Fingers that feel at home playing ivory keys
Making wonderful music
Most of all she is there when you need her

Susannah Knowles 1996

Good Luck

Good luck for the future
For all exams you take
Remember not to work too hard
Especially after eight
Don't start working 'til you've had
Your daily chocolate bar
Remember to eat lots of fish
Then you will go far!
Take lots of breaks to watch TV
To clear your brain from sense
Daily soaps and films to see
None of this revision nonsense
Keep your bedroom tidy and clean
You can't work in a mess
Take lengthy walks to get fresh air
What's five minutes less?
And maybe just the night before
Take a minute with your books
But don't get stressed just take it cool
It can't be as hard as it looks?

Anon 1996

27

When I Awake

In the morning I awake
Usually to a dismal day
Nevertheless my day is complete
When I set my eyes upon you

In the morning I awake
Sometimes to the beauty and wonder of you
On these mornings my heart is filled with joy

In the morning I awake
Looking forward to seeing you

Anon 1996

The Truth

If I weep weep weep
I can't sleep sleep sleep.
If I die die die
I can't cry cry cry.

Bryony 1997

Friendship

At the moment
I'm on the mend
I'm lucky to have
Such a close friend.
Her name is Emma Joce
She understands the most.

Bryony 1997

Reflections

I enjoy watching the sunrise
Seeing the start of the day
Sitting in a field of green grass
Daisies among the occasional thistles
Birds fly overhead
Soaring in their freedom
A solitary rabbit crosses my path
It cautiously turns to meet my glare
I wonder if my look is giving away
All the hurt in the real world today

Bryony 1997

Atlantic College

Atlantic college was such great fun
The weather was good with lots of sun
I made friends who were excited like me
We talked and gossiped over our tea

I had a great time – thanks TOPS a lot
Let's go again and give it a shot! (Archery!)

Bryony 1997

No Matter What

Love prevails no matter what
In times of hard
In times of old
Love has always been revealed

Love prevails no matter what
In time this will be true
Forgive me for my sins
As my love is true

Anon 1997

Just Thinking

It's so peaceful here
Nothing interrupts the silence
Sitting looking and waiting
For nothing in particular
It's nice

The quietness of it all is surprising
Sitting looking and waiting
For anything to happen

Is it?

Overlooking the beautiful sea
So blue and so vast
The long grass and the pretty flowers
Blowing in the wind
Which is not strong
But I can feel this wind
And I just sit look and wait

Bryony 1998

Sisterly Love

It hurts me that she's so distant
It seems she's never in pain and never cries
I wish she could let it go
And tell me what she feels
Life's sometimes hard
But that's how it is

I love her so much
I wish that she knew
Before it's too late
Because my feelings are true

Please, I wish for my sister back
And everything that comes with her
If this wish comes true
I'll be in debt forever to you

Bryony 1998

35

Cancer

Cancer
A word that is feared
Not knowing what lies ahead
Can destroy a life
Everyone hopes for the best
Remission – then recovery?

Bryony 1998

My Life

I am lacing my shoes
I am lacing my corset
I am lacing my life

I am tying my hair
I am tying my dress
I am tying my life

I am making my matches
I am making no money
I am making my life

I am holding my basket
I am holding my basket
I am holding my life

Emma Joce 1998

The Monument You Make

Bryony
Before life begins
A child is given a very carefully selected package of
problems
These
Are yours alone
No one else may have the blessings these problems will
bring you
And only you
Have the special talents and abilities
That will be needed
To triumph and make these problems your servants
The monument you make of your life
Will be a symbol of your love for life itself

Anon 1998

Hide & Seek

There is happiness
You have to look seek and find.
A moment of panic
Who what where?
It will all become clear tomorrow
But will tomorrow ever come?

Bryony 1999

Feelings

First shock and numbness
Hoping it's not here again.
Thoughts of disbelief and many lies
Finally news of the truth.
Many tears
Anger then pain.

Bryony 1999

Listening

Words being spoken
Calming and gentle words.
Almost a whisper
A conversation I think.

Bryony 1999

Reality

Floating in water
Weightless in space
Walking on land
Living on Earth.
One human being among many
Living together along with others.
Village town city
It may be small or large.
A country with variation
In everyone and everything.
We are one planet among many
One solar system among thousands
Our galaxy the Milky Way
Only one of millions.

Bryony 1999

Chances

A chance that she has been given
She is lucky to have that chance
Simply destroyed by a moment of desperation
It may be right it may be wrong
I long for that chance
Hope will keep me hoping for it

Bryony 1999

The Closing Of An Open Door

Feelings of sadness around
Some joy from the gathering
Happiness was present but only a little

An aura of mourning secreted in the air
Something had died
Remembering the times that were good
Remembering the times that were not

Thinking of those that had seen this idea
Just a creation seen as pure and simple
This was the beginning of knowledge forever

Bryony 1999

Equilibrium

Religion is like driving
Or is driving like religion?
I'm going to run over it then crash
Crash into religion as a victim.

I believe in flowers
I believe in sunshine and joy
I believe there is good and evil
I believe in forgiving and forgetting
I believe in living life to the full.

Bryony 1999

Sounds of the World

Birds singing in the morning sunshine
A distant ring of church bells
The engines of rush hour traffic
Sounds of music classical pop jazz
People walking and talking
The piercing tone of a mobile phone
A child crying
Another in his pushchair fast asleep
An aeroplane flies overhead
No one seems to notice
The splash made from a jump into a puddle
The cash machine bleeping to say it's empty
A friend passing says Hello her pace is brisk
Shopping supermarkets the rustling of plastic bags
This is everyday life
Life as we know it to be

Bryony 1999

I Am and I Feel

I feel different
I am different
I feel strange
I am strange
I feel relieved
I am relieved
I feel tired today
I am tired today
I'll feel better tomorrow
I am going to feel better tomorrow
I feel quite lucky at the moment
I am feeling lucky today
I feel like I'm on top of the world
I am on top of the world
I feel like somebody special
I am somebody special
I am who I am
I am me

Bryony 1999

47

Jigsaw Puzzle

It's strange that she's not here
A spirit that has been lost
I can talk to her soon
Maybe that will bring us the truth

I can hear her voice
Her music in the background
Life is not one
It feels less than one

When will I be 'whole' again?
A person with all the parts
Hopefully a piece will come into this place
This place is reserved for her
Only she fits this part

Bryony 1999

In memory of Hayley Joanne Rowett
(b. 22nd March 1982; d.10th March 1999)
who lost her battle against cancer

Today

Today was a good day
Realisation came and 'bang'
It hit me right in the face
I knew really if I am honest

Today was good day
I spoke to my sister and to my father
I had dinner with my mother
I helped a friend who was in need

Today was a good day
The sun was shining but there was a soft wind
I thought about things special things
Tomorrow will also be a good day

Bryony 1999

Sarah H

So happy all the time
A friend who is young but mature
Too grown up for her age
Please let her be young again
Do childhood things
And play childhood games
I am glad she is my friend
My glimmer of light at the end of the tunnel

Bryony 1999

Flower

Like a flower blowing in the wind
So delicate and fresh
Having a fragrance as protection

Walls surround her presence
Never be tempted to look inside
For there exists a human being
A person from somewhere
Most likely a place that wants to be forgotten

Bryony 1999

Remembering

Remembering is a strange thing
You remember what people say and do
You remember the past
You think about the future
What will be surprised upon us?
What do we have to face?
I remember being young
Now I am reminded that I am older

Bryony 1999

Christmas

Soon it will be Christmas
A time to rejoice and be happy
Time to think about the year gone past
The good and the bad

Remembering people
What they are doing
And who they are

Stop to think about life
Are we living or dead?

Next year my new life begins
Free from pain, heartbreak and worry
I will be young again
Have nice dreams not nightmares
I will be a new person
A new Bryony

Bryony 1999

Expectation

An expectation of hope
Tomorrow, a day of belief
Sometimes things may work
Others are destined to fail
One thing in your life is for sure
Remembering that you are you

Bryony 1999

Sixth Sense

There are just too many things to do
I'm not much help to you
Please tell me that I make no sense
Comfort me and take away the pretence

Thoughts travel in and around my mind
Believing one day that I may find
A world that has no bad
Somewhere, I know this place does exist

When I find this special place
I'll say 'hello', so he'll know my face
Hoping one day you'll all come and join me
But for now this is where I should be

I do not ask for much in life
One day I may become a husband's wife
I would love to hear my own baby cry
But a sacrifice was made
So my own life wasn't to die

Bryony 1999

Cat – Dog

Like mother, like daughter
A fairytale well understood

Like father, like son
A thought rather than a story

Like sister, like brother
A spark well lit

Like one twin, like the other
A close relationship, well formed

Like husband, like wife
A marriage, well bound

Like boy, like girl
A difference well known

Like cat, like dog
Not human but still living

Bryony 1999

How Long?

You sit there
Looking so sad
As if wondering
What might have been

I feel that no words
Can comfort you
But I try my best
To pull you out of deep despair

It breaks my heart
To see you like this
A shadow of your former self
I feel so helpless

They say time heals all wounds
How long will it take
Before you are again
Who you used to be

Susannah Knowles 1999

57

Millennium

May this year be a good one
If this is so
Let the world be fair and free from pain
Let us all have peace
Encourage to listen
Not ignore problems that exist
New ideas
Inside and out
Use our knowledge
Make this world a better place

Bryony 2000

Memories

She was my friend
Someone to talk to when times were hard
She still is my friend
Just not here in person anymore
But present
In her own happy and kind spirit

Bryony 2000

In memory of Katy Rachel Frankish
(b. 2nd April 1986; d. 22nd February 2000)
who lost her battle against cancer.

59

Deceit

A web of deceit
A string of lies
A question needed to be asked
An answer needed to be given

The truth was to be known
Speak your words and your wisdom
To everyone
To all and sundry

Can we now live in harmony?
Altogether as one
Can we forgive and forget?
The past is now history
And the living can survive forever

Bryony 2000

A Day May Pass

A day may pass
When times seem bad

A week may open people's eyes
Eyes which long to be shut

A month may broaden these horizons
And let love and hope embrace the world

Bryony 2000

The Summer Sun

Our cherry red faces
Our crimson red bodies
All things bared to the sky
A sign that tells us
Summer is here

In a few days
This brightness may fade
It may disappear forever

How sad it is
To have such a thing
Appear and then vanish
It must be a sign to say
'Look at me
I am your sun
And part of your summer'
But in truth is it saying
'Goodbye, I'll see you next year?'

Bryony 2000

Peace

I don't want to get up and out of my bed
And face the world today
Why? asks my mother

It's so cruel, wicked, so bitter and twisted

There was a time when
There was laughter and joy
Albeit short lived

We ask that peace
Be here with us all
Everyone and everything calm
A wish, that has not yet been granted

Eventually in time
It may become
A reality that enters our world

Bryony 2000

Alphabet Words

A time to remember the past
But also to imagine the future
Clear memories of others
Divide myself into two
Eating away at my conscience
Forever, but never forgotten
Girls against boys in a race
Holding the answer high in the air
In a moment the silence is broken
Just like a falcon and its prey
Knowing there will be pain
Let there be love and peace
Man and woman as one
Not as two
Open your eyes to the truth
Perhaps this is a sign
Quite obviously
Remember that word
Say it out loud
Try, eventually it will come
Usually in another form
Visually it's a place

Where play is abundant
X-Rays await
Yes, another year has passed
Zodiac sign Taurus in May

Bryony 2000

Invader

Everyday I remember the cancer
How it came and invaded my body
It didn't ask if I minded
Having something inside me
Replicating
In each little orifice
In every tiny space
How rude!
Just barging in
And making itself known
Regardless

Gradually it made friends
Played with others
Turning them against me
They were all friends now
Bullying and scheming
To evict me from this world
I was helpless on my own
Was my body mine or their's?
I needed help

Physical pain was suffered
Harm was done
But most important
The internal invaders destroyed

Now we were winning
Survival in sight
Help in relieving this burden of life
My morbidity stayed

Preserved for the future
The invaders repelled
Justice has been served

Bryony 2000

On The Shelf

I can shake rattle and roll
Just like a toy for sale in a shop
No price can match the gift of your life
If I am sold I cannot survive
But if I remain on the shelf
I can see a future

Bryony 2001

Evol – A Mirror Image

Wherever there is love
There is pain
A pain that cannot be hidden
Or understood
Love is a word that absorbs hope
Anticipation of things ahead

It's a love that can never be lost
A person never to be replaced
A special bond between two lovers
A bond that can never be broken
But can melt into nothing

Days of silence
Hour upon hour alone
Taking minutes just to remember the past
Seconds of doubt

From one we became two
Division of this love is too unique
A love that can be no more
Something harsh
Has burst this bubble of hope

Bryony 2003

A Poisonous Flower

Bryony
A poisonous flower
Yet not so poisonous in person
A person of courage strength and feeling
One I could love no more.
Bryony, a very special person to all

Anon 2003